Prophets
or Profits?

A journey through Advent

Prophets
or Profits?

A journey through Advent

15 assemblies for secondary schools

Mike Anderson

Illustrations by Paul Heesome

Kevin
Mayhew

First published in 2001 by KEVIN MAYHEW LTD
Buxhall, Stowmarket, Suffolk IP14 3BW
Email: info@kevinmayhewltd.com

The material in this book first appeared in
The Complete Assembly Resource Book

9 8 7 6 5 4 3 2 1 0

ISBN 1 84003 784 9
Catalogue No 1500449

Illustrations by Paul Heesome
Cover design by Jonathan Stroulger
Typeset by Elisabeth Bates

Contents

This project is dedicated to our mums – each of whom is a one-woman promotion and marketing department for her son!

Overview

This project is based on a series of 15 posters. The idea is to create a sort of Advent calendar by adding a poster to classroom walls each day over the last three weeks of the Advent term. With each poster is a 'thought for the day' which could be read by either teacher or pupils together with a daily prayer. (On page 38 a larger copy of the prayer used each day is provided for the wall.)

The materials can be used in a variety of ways:

- A number of the 'thoughts for the day' could be selected to form the basis of an Advent service.

- The illustrations could be photocopied onto OHP transparencies to be used in an assembly hall or chapel.

- The illustrations are modelled around a trinity of images and tones – some icons having specific parts to play. Identifying what each of them symbolises may form the basis of a discussion.

- The illustrations could be a springboard for a more penetrating study of the use of number and image symbolism so traditional in religious art.

- Considering the roles may be the starting point for an empathetic written piece, pupils taking on the role of one of the figures in a particular illustration.

- This in turn could lead to a piece of drama.

- Classes could reflect on the images, suggesting an appropriate symbolic mood colour for the message, e.g. a colour to reflect celebration, conflict, joy or hope.

- Pupils could be invited to design their own trinity of images to form the basis of a greetings card.

- Although devised for use in schools, this project can be adapted for use in churches and Sunday school.

Whichever way the materials are used, we hope that in some way participants will have the opportunity to more powerfully experience the wonderful liturgical season that is Advent.

Today's poster is entitled

Are you ready?

Thought for the day

The Advent term in schools is very often the time for the school's Open Night. Can you remember the last time you were preparing for Open Night?

Everyone is involved in some way, whether it is doing work for the displays, training to be a guide, practising dancing, playing and singing or even just keeping out of the teachers' way and getting on with work set.

So often, Open Night is a really successful event, and one of the main reasons for the success is the tremendous amount of preparation that goes into it. There's an old saying: 'If we fail to plan – we plan to fail!' It might sound corny but there's a ring of truth to it.

Advent is the time to plan for the coming of Jesus. But what do you plan for? Is it the giving of presents? Do you and your family plan for mega-meals and parties? These things are all fine and can be good, but if we lose the REASON for the SEASON – all of these are essentially fruitless and pointless.

So, as we make our journey through Advent – let's wake up to the excitement of a new baby coming into our family. Let's wake up to the opportunities for building bridges that Christmas gives us. Let's wake up to get ready to put the Christ back into Christmas.

A few seconds of silent reflection

Daily prayer (said together):

Lord, we've walked in darkness too long.
We wait for the light of your love
to shine on us once more –
guiding, warming and protecting.
Lord, we wait for you! Amen.

1: Are you ready?

Today's poster is entitled

Prophets or profits?

Thought for the day

It is often thought that a prophet is someone who tells the future, but, in the Bible, the prophets do a great deal more than think and talk about the future. Generally, they looked back to the 'good old days' when all was well with God's Chosen People. Then they contrasted this with any bad things that were happening in their lifetime, reflecting that things weren't what they used to be. Only then did they consider the future – outlining how wonderful it would be when God's kingdom was fully established, but adding a warning as to what might happen if the people did not mend their ways.

So, prophets deal with the past, present and the future.

Christmas decorations up in October! Christmas cards with snow on! Christmas cards with robins on! Christmas cards with the Simpsons on! Pester the adults for your presents: Mobile phones! PCs! Furbies! Slade blaring out 'It's Chriiiiiistmaaaaaaaas!' Turkey! Stuffing! Biggest bar of chocolate in the world! 'We wish you a merry Christmas!' Drink, drink, drink! Money, money, money! Buy, buy, buy! Profits! Profits! Profits!

What will your Christmas be about – PROPHETS or PROFITS?

A few seconds of silent reflection

Daily prayer (said together):

Lord, we've walked in darkness too long.
We wait for the light of your love
to shine on us once more –
guiding, warming and protecting.
Lord, we wait for you! Amen.

2: Prophets or profits?

Mary – Y9

Thought for the day

We tend to think of Mary, the mother of Jesus, as a radiant, beautiful lady – always smiling and ever patient. Artists over the centuries have tended to depict her as the epitome of perfection, with white and blue robes, a halo and a tendency to hover a few feet off the ground!

However, when you think about the reality that Mary faced, you start to realise what a tough time she went through. First of all, it's likely that Mary was only about 14 years old when the Angel Gabriel appeared to her. That's roughly the age of our Year 9 pupils. Not only did she have the shock and surprise of an angel appearing to her, she also had the task of explaining it all to her parents.

Can you imagine it? Mary comes down the stairs and says: 'Oh, Mum and Dad, I've got something to tell you.'
Mum replies, 'Oh, what's that, Mary?' Dad is not really listening – too busy reading the local news scroll!
  'I'm going to have a baby!'
  'You're what?!?!' Dad's listening now!
  'I'm going to have a baby.'
Now Dad's really angry: 'Who's the father – I'll kill him! Is it that Joseph?'
  'No, Dad, it's God himself by the power of the Holy Spirit.'
  'Have you been drinking?' Dad asks. 'I've never heard such nonsense in all my life! Who told you to say that?'
Mary replies, 'The Angel Gabriel, Dad . . . Dad? . . . Dad? . . .' But Dad does not reply because he's passed out.

Mary was one tough young girl who would have had to cope with village gossips and people laughing behind her back. Maybe we should remember her as a determined and resilient teenager, with the same sorts of feelings as teenagers today, who was chosen to do something really special for God. Is there something less spectacular that God has chosen for you?

A few seconds of silent reflection

Daily prayer (said together):

Lord, we've walked in darkness too long.
We wait for the light of your love
to shine on us once more –
guiding, warming and protecting.
Lord, we wait for you! Amen.

Angel!

Thought for the day

We heard yesterday how the Angel Gabriel appeared to the teenage Mary. But what do we know about angels? When you were younger, were you ever called 'a little angel'? It's the sort of thing doting parents, and particularly grandparents, say, isn't it?

What do *you* think of when you hear the word 'angel'? Is it chubby little babies draped with fine white silk, playing harps in the clouds? Is it androgynous beings, dressed in white, with enormous wings? What do angels look like?

The simple answer is that we don't know! But if we do a little detective work, we can say something about angels. If you look through the Bible, you'll find that almost every time an angel appears to an individual, the first words the angel says are: 'Don't be afraid!' If these are the first words, the logical conclusion to this is that angels must be absolutely terrifying!

So, we can guess that they must look frightening, but what is their purpose? Basically, they are messengers sent by God. They are biblical 'Kissograms' if you like. They pass on messages which are often surprising – surely none more so than the news that Mary was pregnant. They are also sent sometimes to protect and guide people.

Have you ever been an angel? Have you ever encouraged someone to believe in Jesus or are you too afraid to admit to others that you pray or believe? Have you ever looked after someone who needed help? You probably have – be that angel to someone today!

A few seconds of silent reflection

Daily prayer (said together):

Lord, we've walked in darkness too long.
We wait for the light of your love
to shine on us once more –
guiding, warming and protecting.
Lord, we wait for you! Amen.

4: Angel!

Today's poster is entitled

Emmanuel

Thought for the day

In the Gospel of Matthew, five prophecies are mentioned as being fulfilled by Jesus in the first two chapters. One of these is: 'A virgin shall conceive and give birth to a son – and he shall be called Emmanuel.'

The name 'Emmanuel' means 'God is with us'.

Have you ever had an Emmanuel moment when you've felt God close to you? If you have, it may have been during a time of trouble – a family difficulty or bereavement. Such moments are really precious and should be treasured.

There was once a man who had died and was looking back on his life as a journey with God. Through most of his life, he could see two sets of footprints in the sand and he said to God, 'I can see you were there with me – on my journey.' He noticed though that during the most rocky and difficult periods of his life, there was only one set of footprints and he said to God: 'Why did you abandon me when times were hard?' God answered: 'My son, when times were hard and you see only one set of footprints – that was when I carried you!'

You don't get Emmanuel moments just in church or at assemblies. They can happen any time, any place, anywhere. Give yourself a chance to experience God. Give yourself space; stop for just a few minutes when you get home tonight and let God carry you.

A few seconds of silent reflection

Daily prayer (said together):

Lord, we've walked in darkness too long.
We wait for the light of your love
to shine on us once more –
guiding, warming and protecting.
Lord, we wait for you! Amen.

Joseph – forgotten hero!

Thought for the day

Joseph is the forgotten hero of the Christmas story. In the school nativity play he only gets to say, 'We are weary travellers – have you any room at your inn?'

In some school nativity plays even the sheep and cows get higher billing than Joseph! And yet, he was quite an amazing man.

Remember, he was engaged to Mary and she became pregnant. It is important to remember that, in those days, to be pregnant before you were married was considered scandalous. Joseph knew it was not his child, but he did not abandon Mary. When she told him it was God's child, he did not say she was round the twist. When the gossips were saying things about him and Mary, he stood by her.

When he and Mary were travelling to Bethlehem, you can appreciate that Mary – being heavily pregnant – would have got all the attention. When the wise men came to see Jesus, Joseph would not have been in the frame.

And yet, Joseph was the one who gave up his home and became a refugee with Mary and Jesus, in order to escape the massacre of the innocents at Bethlehem. Joseph was the one who worked as a carpenter to provide for Mary and Jesus – all the while knowing that Jesus was not his son. He would not have been human had he not had doubts at some times in his life about Mary's story of the Angel Gabriel. True, an angel did appear to Joseph in a dream – but would he have questioned this? How did he deal with all the doubts and upset he must have felt? Perhaps Joseph's theme song would have been 'Search for the hero inside yourself'.

Joseph – the forgotten hero who did find himself!

A few seconds of silent reflection

Daily prayer (said together):

Lord, we've walked in darkness too long.
We wait for the light of your love
to shine on us once more –
guiding, warming and protecting.
Lord, we wait for you! Amen.

6: Joseph – forgotten hero!

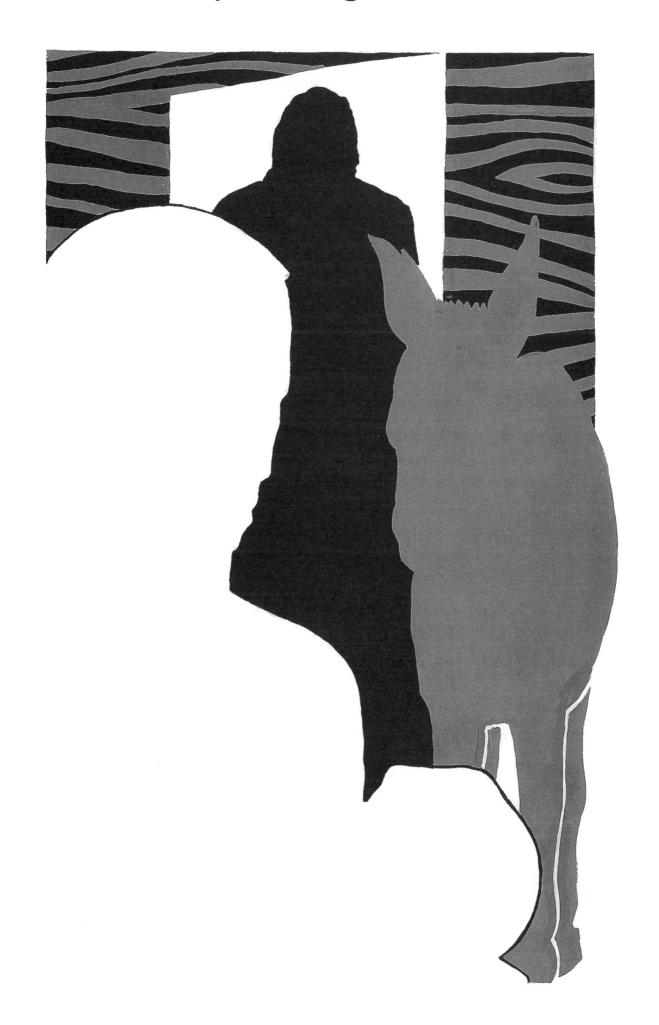

Today's poster is entitled

Census

Thought for the day

Every 10 years in Britain a nation-wide census takes place. The information gathered from it is essential in ensuring the country can plan for the future as regards the building of hospitals and schools. It helps government to plan for the training of a variety of essential professions. The first census in this country was in 1086, ordered by William the Conqueror – the result of it was *The Domesday Book*.

However, the Roman Empire had conducted surveys over a thousand years earlier. One of these was ordered by the Emperor Augustus (after whom, incidentally, the month of August is named) and the census was used by Roman officials to decide how much tax to levy on the people of the Empire. These surveys were far from popular. For a start each man had to go back, with his family, to his ancestors' home town. Where would you have to go?

In Joseph's case this meant a journey of over 100 kilometres, from Nazareth to Bethlehem. That is a considerable distance to have to walk, and you can imagine how awkward it would have been for the heavily pregnant Mary to make this journey. It would have taken four or five days – four or five days without even the basic home comforts; four or five days of carrying all they might need in case the baby was born; four or five days of either camping out or asking people to put them up (not a Little Chef or Trust House Forte in sight!); four or five days of wondering if their baby was going to be born on the road.

Many infant school nativity plays include the song 'Little donkey' but it doesn't really capture the discomfort, cold and fatigue that Mary and Joseph must have suffered. As we make our journey through Advent, let's remember that, for Joseph and Mary, it was not an exciting journey, but a stressful and exhausting one.

A few seconds of silent reflection

Daily prayer (said together):

Lord, we've walked in darkness too long.
We wait for the light of your love
to shine on us once more –
guiding, warming and protecting.
Lord, we wait for you! Amen.

7: Census

Bethlehem

Thought for the day

The word 'Bethlehem' literally means 'house of bread', and it was here that the 'Bread of Life' – Jesus – was born. Even before the birth of Jesus, the town had great religious significance. It was the birthplace of the great Jewish leader, David. Indeed, Bethlehem became known as the town of David.

David was only a boy when God guided the prophet Samuel to him. His most famous exploit was the slaying of Goliath. At that time, battles were sometimes settled by letting the champions of the respective armies fight it out. The army whose champion won was then deemed to have won the battle. The enemies of the Israelites (David's people) were the Philistines. Their champion was Goliath – who was 9 feet 8 inches tall (that's about 3 feet taller than the basketball player, Michael Jordan). Not surprisingly, the Israelite king, Saul, had a few problems in finding anyone willing to take Goliath on. Eventually David volunteered. Saul gave David his own suit of armour, but the boy David, having put it on, found it so big and heavy that he couldn't walk, so he took it off and approached Goliath without armour or sword. When Goliath saw David, he started laughing – until a stone fired from David's sling hit him on the forehead, penetrated the skull and knocked him to the ground. David then picked up Goliath's sword and cut his head off.

David went on to become a great king. He was a gifted musician and wrote many songs, now recorded in the Bible in the book of Psalms. It is no surprise that the Israelites wanted another leader like David, and the prophets Isaiah and Micah said that this long-awaited Messiah would be born in Bethlehem. Bethlehem was and still is the focus of the Israelites' hope for the future.

Christians today sing the carol 'O little town of Bethlehem' and echo this sense of hope in the words:
The hopes and fears of all the years are met in thee tonight.

A few seconds of silent reflection

Daily prayer (said together):

Lord, we've walked in darkness too long.
We wait for the light of your love
to shine on us once more –
guiding, warming and protecting.
Lord, we wait for you! Amen.

8: Bethlehem

Today's poster is entitled

How many? How wise?

Thought for the day

Have you ever gone carol singing or had carol singers at your door? If you have, you will know the carol:

> *We three kings of Orient are;*
> *bearing gifts we travel afar. . .*

This is actually rather inaccurate. Firstly, the visitors from the East were probably astrologers rather than kings and, secondly, there is no mention in the Gospels of how many there were. It is a long-standing church tradition that there must have been three because three gifts were brought, and a mosaic created in the sixth century even named them as Balthazar, Melchior and Caspar. However, this is probably speculation.

Were these astrologers – probably from the country we now call Iraq – the first century's answer to 'Dipstick Meg'? Nowadays, horoscopes are usually seen as a bit of fun, but at the time of these wise men, astrologers were well respected. They underwent years of training and some of the discoveries they made about the stars astound today's scientists.

Collectively they are also sometimes referred to as the Magi – from which we get the word 'magic'. So, what drove these educated men to follow a star? The desire to see the baby who would grow to be king was strong within them. They travelled hundreds of miles to meet Jesus.

Do you want to meet Jesus this Christmas?

A few seconds of silent reflection

Daily prayer (said together):

Lord, we've walked in darkness too long.
We wait for the light of your love
to shine on us once more –
guiding, warming and protecting.
Lord, we wait for you! Amen.

9: How many? How wise?

Ships of the desert

Thought for the day

Yesterday we heard about the wise men from the East. Let's spare a thought today for the beasts of burden which carried them and their entourage.

Known as 'ships of the desert', camels stand about six feet tall at the shoulders and can have either one or two humps, depending on the breed. Camels have the ability to go without water for several days. They can survive such hardship because they have special pouches in the stomach which can hold water to be released when required. Their humps are stores of flesh and fat, which means they can survive without food for long periods.

Camels are ideally adapted to travelling across desert landscapes. They have very long eyelashes, which protect their eyes in sandstorms. They also have the ability to close their nostrils. Camels have an acute sense of smell and can detect where water is. They are incredibly strong and can carry loads as big as 450 kilograms (1000 pounds/70-plus stone). They travel at a pace of about 2.5 miles per hour and can walk for up to 12 hours a day.

So what can we learn from camels? Sometimes we have to carry big burdens – emotional burdens – and we think there will never be an end to our problems. But we dig deep and somehow come through. Our lives are sometimes difficult journeys, but we are sustained by an inner strength, until we experience 'oasis moments' in our lives when we are refreshed by someone's act of kindness or love. And then the burden seems lighter and the journey easier.

Make it your challenge today to provide an 'oasis moment' for someone else.

A few seconds of silent reflection

Daily prayer (said together):

Lord, we've walked in darkness too long.
We wait for the light of your love
to shine on us once more –
guiding, warming and protecting.
Lord, we wait for you! Amen.

10: Ships of the desert

Star

Thought for the day

The wise men were said to have followed a star to Bethlehem. The idea of following a star is quite perplexing, because it is so far from our everyday experience – it sounds like something from *The X-Files*.

Many people have tried to find explanations for this star. These go from the plain wacky – such as, the star was an alien spacecraft – to the scientific – for example, the star was a visitation from Haley's Comet which orbits the earth every 76 years. However, it is difficult to reconcile such theories with Matthew's Gospel, which records that 'the star went forward and halted over the place where the child was.' Does a comet stop over a particular town? Maybe it was quite simply a miracle.

Another possible explanation lies in the way in which ancient writers reported the births of great historical figures. The birth of Julius Caesar, for example, was preceded by the appearance of a star, according to Roman writings. Similarly, it is recorded that a star appeared at the time of the birth of Alexander the Great. Could it be that the writer of Matthew's Gospel wanted to emphasise the importance of the birth of Jesus and so included the appearance of a celestial body? Such a literary device makes it clear that the birth of Jesus was an extraordinary event.

And this is the essence of the story of the birth of Jesus. Jesus was human like us and yet, at the same time, was the Son of God. The unexplained, mysterious star is just one aspect of the astounding story of his birth.

A few seconds of silent reflection

Daily prayer (said together):

Lord, we've walked in darkness too long.
We wait for the light of your love
to shine on us once more –
guiding, warming and protecting.
Lord, we wait for you! Amen.

Three gifts

Thought for the day

In England it has become a tradition for the Queen to offer gifts of gold, frankincense and myrrh at the altar of the Chapel Royal at St James' Palace, on the feast of the Epiphany.

But what are you planning to give this Christmas? For Christians, the emphasis should be on the giving of gifts, as we re-enact the giving of gifts by the wise men to Jesus. In some countries, Christmas gifts are exchanged on 6 January – the feast of the Epiphany. Would you be able to wait that long?

The gifts you get will tell us something about you. They may tell us that you support a certain football team, or like a particular pop group. They may tell us that you watch a certain TV programme, or like to choose your own clothes. So what of the gifts the wise men gave? What do they tell us about Jesus?

Firstly, gold: this was a gift traditionally given to kings. It emphasises that Jesus came to be a KING.

Secondly, frankincense: this is made from various gum resins, which, when burned, give off a strong fragrance. As the frankincense burns, the smoke rises and this is a symbol for Christians of their prayers rising to God. It emphasises Jesus' role as a PRIEST who was to lead people in prayer and towards God.

Finally, myrrh: again taken from the gum of certain trees. Myrrh was used as an oil for rubbing on the body, and was particularly used when people were close to death. A modern-day equivalent would be the oils used in aromatherapy. It emphasises that Jesus came to suffer and die like the PROPHETS before him.

JESUS – King, priest and prophet.

A few seconds of silent reflection

Daily prayer (said together):

Lord, we've walked in darkness too long.
We wait for the light of your love
to shine on us once more –
guiding, warming and protecting.
Lord, we wait for you! Amen.

12: Three gifts

Candle in the wind

Thought for the day

One of the most haunting aspects of the television coverage of Princess Diana's death was a report from outside Buckingham Palace, where people gathered one evening, holding lighted candles, and laying flowers at the Palace gates. The symbol of the candle continued with Elton John's reworking of the song 'Candle in the wind', originally written for Marilyn Monroe.

In the midst of a society where electricity lights our streets and homes, the symbolic power of the naked flickering flame of a candle is still immense.

For Christians, the lighted candle is a reminder that Jesus is the Light of the World – the one who guides us through the dark moments of life. As the new Church year starts, we light candles on Advent wreaths. Three of the candles are purple, a colour signifying the need to repent (turn over a new leaf) – and one is pink, as a sign of the joy we share at the birth of the baby Jesus.

When a child is baptised, a lighted candle is given to the parents as a reminder that Jesus should be the light which guides the child as it develops.

When a person dies, we often light candles for them. We look on the gently flickering flame, and somehow it helps us to pray.

This Christmas, try to take the opportunity to help someone who is having a bad time. Take the opportunity to pray for someone. Take the opportunity to . . .

. . . light a candle in the darkness.

A few seconds of silent reflection

Daily prayer (said together):

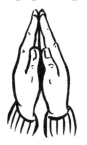

Lord, we've walked in darkness too long.
We wait for the light of your love
to shine on us once more –
guiding, warming and protecting.
Lord, we wait for you! Amen.

13: Candle in the wind

Shepherds

Thought for the day

The birth of Jesus is recorded in only two of the four Gospels – Matthew and Luke. In Matthew's account, the first people to visit Jesus are the Magi, or wise men. They bring rather grand gifts – gold, frankincense and myrrh.

In contrast, Luke records that the birth of Jesus is announced to shepherds out in the fields, looking after their sheep. This suggests that it was summer, and the shepherds had had to move further away from their usual grazing grounds to find food for their animals. It was quite usual for the shepherds to stay with the sheep in the fields when they were far from home.

You probably already know that shepherds were somewhat looked down upon at the time of Jesus. Jesus even made a bit of a joke about one in the parable of the Lost Sheep. It is significant, therefore, that the birth of the Messiah – the Son of God – was revealed to these poor shepherds. It is an indication that Jesus himself was to take an *option for the poor* – that he regarded all people as being *equal in dignity*.

This is a tremendous challenge for us. Maybe we can't make big dramatic gestures, like giving gold to the poor; but why not take the chance this Advent to do something for someone less fortunate than ourselves?

Feeding people's spirits is just as important as feeding their bodies – making them feel valued. Perhaps there is an old person living alone near you and this Christmas, with your parents' permission, you can make a visit and just chat with them and make them feel they are still valued in the community.

A few seconds of silent reflection

Daily prayer (said together):

Lord, we've walked in darkness too long.
We wait for the light of your love
to shine on us once more –
guiding, warming and protecting.
Lord, we wait for you! Amen.

14: Shepherds

New life!

Thought for the day

And so, we have reached the last day of our journey through Advent, and we think about the birth of Jesus. As with every child, it was a miracle. As with every child, it brought great happiness. As with every child, there was sadness to follow at some point in his life.

But, for today, let's focus on the joy of new life. Forget about the nappies and sleepless nights. Think about the first smile, the first word, the first step!

And let's use it as a chance to start again ourselves. Let's throw off the cloaks of being 'cool', reserved and cold. Let's put on garments of joy, laughter and smiles. It may be cold over Christmas, but let's remember we are not God's frozen people – we are God's chosen people!

Let's enjoy the last day of our journey. If there are any relationships which need to be put right, take the chance to do it, so there's no chance for bitterness to develop over the Christmas season.

During the holidays, enjoy life and help others to enjoy it, too. We are celebrating one of the most momentous events in history – only Easter surpasses it, from the Christian point of view. So, celebrate – celebrate your friends, your family, your school – but above all, celebrate the birth of that baby, who cried aloud in a stable, some two thousand years ago, in a land far away.

Happy Christmas!

A few seconds of silent reflection

Daily prayer (said together):

Lord, we've walked in darkness too long.
We wait for the light of your love
to shine on us once more –
guiding, warming and protecting.
Lord, we wait for you! Amen.

15: New life!

Lord, we've walked in darkness too long.

We wait for the light of your love

to shine on us once more –

guiding, warming and protecting.

Lord, we wait for you!

Amen.